AF575386

THE MEMOIRS *of*
BLESSED RAMON LLULL

THE FIRST MISSIONARY MARTYR TO THE MUSLIMS

THE MEMOIRS *of*

BLESSED RAMON LLULL

THE FIRST MISSIONARY MARTYR TO THE MUSLIMS

Translated and edited by

Fr. Robert Nixon, OSB

Abbey of the Most Holy Trinity
New Norcia, Western Australia

TAN Books
Gastonia, North Carolina

Translated and edited by Fr. Robert Nixon, OSB

Cover design by Jordan Avery

Cover image: *Representation of Raymond Lulle in Catalan Ramon Llull, Spanish Raimundo Lulio (Lullo) (Lull) philosopher, theologian and poet Catalan (1235-1315)*, c.1618 (oil on canvas) © Iberfoto / Bridgeman Images

Interior image: *Spanish philosopher, layman, scientist, he undertook missionary work in North Africa and Asia Minor* © PVDE / Bridgeman Images

ISBN: 978-1-5051-3525-1
Kindle ISBN: 978-1-5051-3597-8
ePUB ISBN: 978-1-5051-3596-1

Published in the United States by
TAN Books
PO Box 269
Gastonia, NC 28053
www.TANBooks.com

Printed in the United States of America

19th century lithograph of Blessed Ramon Llull. The ribbon coming from his mouth reads *Lux mea est ipse Dominus* (My light is the Lord Himself).

CONTENTS

TRANSLATOR'S INTRODUCTION

BLESSED RAMON LLULL[1] (c.1232–1315), known as the *Doctor Illuminatus*, was a Franciscan tertiary and the first missionary martyr to the Muslims. He was not only a fearless and enterprising proclaimer of the Gospel but also a scholar and thinker of amazing originality and energy. During the course of his exciting life, he made numerous missionary expeditions to northern Africa and traveled over Europe soliciting support for both the conversion of the Saracens and the reclaiming of the Holy Land through a new crusade.

Llull's literary output is phenomenal, and a comprehensive catalogue includes well over three hundred books, most of which are of considerable length. Central to these is his *Greater Art* (*Arts Major*), which bears

[1] The name of the saint is given in a variety of different spellings in both Latin (*Raimundus/Raymundus*) and English (Raymund/Ramon; and Lull/Lully/Llull.) The form used here is that preferred by contemporary scholars.

the subtitle *The Key to All Arts and Sciences and All the Works of the Divine Author.* This fascinating and ambitious work presents a method Llull invented (or rather, received through divine inspiration) for proving or evaluating the truth of any proposition and for obtaining mastery over any field of knowledge. It must be admitted that this work is very difficult to follow and apply, and the saint's own explanations of it are so voluminous (comprising about fifty volumes) that it is not fully or perfectly understood by scholars even to this day.[2]

He wrote on virtually every subject imaginable, including theology, philosophy, jurisprudence, logic, rhetoric, mathematics, astronomy, chemistry, physics, medicine, etc.,[3] drawing extensively upon the science and learning of the Arabs whose language he had diligently mastered. His imagination also extended to the writing of novels of a spiritual nature, and his *Blanquerna*, a fictional account of a merchant who is converted

---

2 Including the present translator!

3 Llull's writings even include works on the production of synthetic gemstones and the mysterious Philosopher's Stone. Such writings reflect that state of science at the time, when there was no distinction between chemistry and alchemy.

and eventually becomes pope, is regarded as the first major work of Catalan literature.

The life of Blessed Ramon Llull presented in this volume is a translation of a remarkable memoir dictated by the saint himself in September 1311 in Paris (just a few years before his death). In some instances, most notably for the description of his final expedition and martyrdom, it has been supplemented by the biography of Blessed Ramon written by Charles de Bovelles, a celebrated French mathematician, philosopher, and theologian of the fifteenth and sixteenth centuries.

The life of Ramon Llull is a fast-paced and thrilling narrative, reading almost like an action novel. The fact that it is his own authentic memoir is particularly important. For it contains honest and touching admissions of his own weakness and struggles (including experiences of doubt, depression, and fear) and also ungarnished reports of his many failures and disappointments (such as his lack of success in gaining support for his plans for the conversion of the Saracens and the launching of a new crusade). Nevertheless, the sanctity, determination, and single-mindedness of the saint shine through in inspiring fashion. Though he encountered much discouragement, tribulation, and peril, he never allowed himself to be swayed from the work to which Christ had called him.

One of the striking features of Llull's memoir is the degree of respect he exhibits for the Saracen peoples, and also the fairness and goodness he encounters from many of them. Although he did not hesitate to point out the errors of their creed, he did so with such wisdom, courtesy, and logic that he won many of them over to Christianity. In his interest in philosophical theology, logic, and science, he found much to discuss with Arabic scholars and thinkers. Even many of those whom he did not succeed in converting came to respect him and his learning, and his life was spared on more than one occasion because of this. On the other hand, the Papal Curia apparently showed minimal or no interest in his efforts or plans to propagate the Faith. It is to be noted that this was during the era of Avignon popes, when the Catholic Church was wrought with many internal problems of its own.

Included also in this volume is a translation of substantial extracts from Llull's *Libellus de Fine* (*Book on the End*),[4] given here the descriptive title of his *Master-*

[4] "The Latin title of the book, Libellus de fine, could be translated in several possible ways as B*ooklet/Small Book about the End/*

plan for the Conversion of Unbelievers and the Reclaiming of the Holy Land. This work, which has never previously been translated into English, gives a detailed outline of his request made to Pope Clement V and the College of Cardinals for the establishment of monastic academies for the training of future missionaries in foreign languages. It also includes his plans for a new military order to reclaim the Holy Lands from Saracen control.

Llull's Latin is clear and energetic, but often quite distinctive and idiomatic. He freely uses terms and expressions borrowed from both vernacular Catalan and from Arabic. The term *Saracen* has generally been retained, but in some instances (depending upon the context), *Muslim* has been used instead. The term *Tartar* has been rendered as *Mongol*, as it was to that ethnic group that the author was referring. In some instances, sentences have been restructured for the sake of clarity. Texts in square brackets [. . .] are editorial additions.

It is the sincere hope of the translator that this work will offer an insight into the adventurous and devout life of Blessed Ramon Llull, a fascinating saint who gave his very life to spread the Gospel that he loved

---

Goal/Purpose and conveys in the original each of these meaning.

so much. The title given to him of *Doctor Illuminatus* is particularly appropriate, for he shone with a radiant brightness in his intelligence, courage, persistence, and above all, in his ardor for Our Lord Jesus Christ, to whom be glory forever and ever.

Fr. Robert Nixon, OSB
Abbey of the Most Holy Trinity,
New Norcia, Western Australia

THE MEMOIR OF BLESSED RAMON LLULL

PREFACE

In the name of JESUS!

To THE HONOR, praise, and love of Jesus Christ alone, Our Lord and God, Ramon, overcome by the entreaties and requests of his beloved friends and fellow religious, has narrated the account of his life which follows, and he has given permission for his narration to be written down.

In this account are to be found details of his conversion, penitence, and the various deeds and adventures of his life to this point.

CHAPTER I

Ramon's conversion from the vanities of the world after a vision of Christ.

RAMON, AN OFFICER of the palace of the king of Majorca, was excessively devoted to the vanities and allurements of this passing world in his youth. Indeed, his favorite occupation was to spend his time writing love songs to various attractive young maidens who happened to catch his eye and his heart. This, indeed, was a very frequent occurrence for him as a young man!

It happened that one night, he was alone in his bedroom sitting by his bed. And he was then engaged (as was his custom) in composing a lyrical ballad to a certain beautiful woman, with whom he was then infatuated. As he mused intently upon coming up with good rhymes for his new love song, he suddenly saw a miraculous vision at his right side. Behold, it was the form of Our Lord and Savior Jesus Christ, raised up as if He was hanging upon the cross!

Ramon was terrified and overwhelmed by this vision and immediately threw his pen and paper down and hid himself within his bed. He shut his eyes firmly and prayed earnestly to the Lord for mercy.

Rising the next morning, he recollected the vision he had seen in the sober light of day. Surely, thought the youth, it was merely a dream or the product of his heated imagination. In fact, Ramon still burned with ardor for the woman with whom he had fallen in love. Therefore, he quickly put aside all thoughts of matters of religion and dismissed the memory of the vision from his mind.

The next night, he once more applied himself to completing his song for the lovely female who had then captured his heart. And again, Christ appeared to him in a vision, just as had happened on the previous night. This time, Ramon was even more terrified than he had been on the first night. He again leapt into his bed, covering himself with his blankets and shutting his eyes firmly. But once more, when the light of morning appeared, he dismissed the vision as a dream or hallucination and returned to his habitual thoughts of worldly love.

Precisely the same thing happened on the third night, and likewise on the fourth and the fifth. Now, by this stage, Ramon was becoming increasingly uneasy and anxious. By the fifth night, after the vision of the crucified Christ had appeared to him, he could no longer find refuge in sleep but spent the whole night tossing and turning. He considered in his mind the meaning of the vision and the way in which it had interrupted and prevented his completion of his song for the woman with whom he was infatuated. What could it mean? At last, the conclusion dawned upon him. Jesus Christ was calling him to abandon the vanities of the world and the desires of the flesh with which he had been hitherto so occupied and to devote himself wholeheartedly to the service of the Lord.

But still he struggled in his heart, for he recognized that his life to this point had been riddled with impiety, laxity, and vanity. "Perhaps," thought he, "I am unworthy to serve the Lord." The next night, he again passed in sleeplessness and perplexity, pondering this question. But then, illuminated by the grace of the Father of Lights, he reflected upon the infinite mercy, patience, and gentleness of Jesus Christ, which He never failed to show to sinners. And thus Ramon understood very clearly and certainly that God willed him to renounce the world and to serve the Lord Christ with all his heart for the remainder of his life.

CHAPTER II

Ramon commits himself to the conversion of the Saracens and makes three resolutions in support of this plan.

HAVING RESOLVED TO turn his back on the allurements of the world and to devote himself wholeheartedly to the service of Christ, Ramon began to consider what would be the manner in which he could do that so that it would be most pleasing to God and most useful to humanity. And it occurred to him that there could be no better way of serving Christ than to commit himself to the conversion of the Saracens. Now, at that time, the Saracens virtually surrounded the whole of Christendom and even threatened invasion and conquest in many parts. In obedience to this noble and holy inspiration, Ramon resolved to apply himself to this great task, even to the point of giving up his very life to achieve it—all for the love and honor of Jesus Christ.

But when he considered this undertaking more closely, he realized that, as yet, he did not possess the knowledge necessary to perform it successfully. For the truth was, until now, he had been somewhat negligent and undisciplined in his scholarly endeavors, and he knew not a single word of Arabic. In fact [while he understood Latin and the vernacular language of Majorca], he only grasped the principles of grammar in their most rudimentary form. And so, he was overcome with sorrow and even began to sink into despair and discouragement.

But although Ramon did not possess the knowledge which was necessary for this great mission, God, who knows all things, certainly did, and the Lord who called him was ready and able to supply whatever was necessary. By a divine illumination, a wonderful idea sprung up in the heart of Ramon, like the golden sun arising at dawn. Inspired by the Holy Spirit and inflamed with the fervent love of Christ, he would write a book—a most magnificent and marvelous book, like no book ever before written by any mortal hand or read by any human eyes—that would convert the Muslim world from the darkness of error and enlighten them with the glorious splendor of the Truth and the noble radiance of the Faith.

But though he had now resolved to produce such a book that would change the world forever, he found himself at a loss when he tried to determine its form, contents, or plan. And again, he fell into discouragement and sadness. He felt gravely frustrated at his lack of knowledge of how to proceed with his plan for converting the Saracens. Nevertheless, the desire and determination to achieve this holy objective only increased in his soul. For heaven poured into his heart a divine inspiration and an unwavering perseverance. He *would* do it, for God Himself had called him to it.

Yet, before he could achieve this, he recognized that his ignorance of the Arabic language would remain an insuperable obstacle unless he could overcome it and master the common idiom of the Muslim peoples. He realized also that without the aid of other like-minded and fervent individuals who had similarly studied the Arabic language, he would be powerless to accomplish very much at all as a missionary. Considering all these difficulties, the idea occurred to him to approach the pope and various Christian kings and princes throughout Europe to solicit their aid and support in establishing a kind of monastery or college. It was his plan that such a monastery would serve as an academy where suitable religious persons could be trained in the languages of the Arabs and other non-Christian nations in order to be properly equipped to share the Truth of the Catholic Faith with them and to take the light of the Gospel to the furthermost corners of the world.

Thus Ramon set for himself three intentions to which he committed himself heart and soul: first, the devotion of all his efforts and powers, and even his very life itself, to the conversion of the Saracens to the Christian Faith; second, the writing of a book that would infallibly refute the errors of non-believers and display the Truths of the Catholic Faith; and, third, the establishment of a monastery or college to provide Christian missionaries with instruction in the Arabic and other non-European languages.

CHAPTER III

Ramon becomes a Franciscan tertiary, embarks on a pilgrimage to various sacred destinations, and attains eminence as a scholar and author in Paris.

Having committed himself solemnly to these three resolutions, Ramon went early the next morning to the local church. There, upon his knees, he poured out fervent prayers, accompanied by tears and sighs. He begged that the Lord Jesus Christ, who had inspired him to this daring and difficult undertaking, would help him to bring it to a successful fulfillment.

Alas, young Ramon persisted in his initial fervor only for a short time. For he had been imbued with all the caprice and vanity of the world. While his intentions were holy and pious, his character remained weak and vacillating. So he spent the following three months in a state of torpor and tepidity, and languor and lethargy. He genuinely wanted to carry out his intention of missionary work, yet somehow continued to procrastinate and delay.

But then the feast of Saint Francis of Assisi arrived, and he was, by the grace of God, impelled into decisive action. For he attended Mass on that auspicious day, and the local bishop, together with some holy Franciscan friars, preached eloquently upon the merits and virtues of this seraphic saint. Ramon's inspiration and fervor was once more stirred up like a glowing flame within his heart. Immediately, he resolved to follow the example of the great Saint Francis. [Enrolling himself as a member of the third order of the Friars Minor,] he sold all his possessions and property and gave the money to the poor, reserving only what was necessary to ensure the continuing welfare of his immediate family and dependents.

Furthermore, he decided to embark at once on a holy pilgrimage of prayer and penance. Setting out in the rustic garb of a poor mendicant friar, he first visited the ancient shrine of the Blessed Virgin in Rocamadour [in southern France] and then proceeded to visit the relics of Saint James in the distant city of Compostela [in Portugal]. Long and arduous were his wanderings, and many were the sacred places to which he fared. All the while, his prayers were continuous and fervent, imploring the mercy and assistance of God for his future missionary work. In particular, he prayed that he might be granted the grace to bring his three holy resolutions to fruition.

After this period of pilgrimage was complete, Ramon returned to his home in Majorca. It was his resolve then to travel to Paris, that great center of learning and scholarship, in order to acquire the erudition which he perceived would be helpful in presenting the Arabs with convincing arguments for the Christian Faith.

Proceeding to Paris, Ramon applied himself to his studies with assiduity.[5] Although, as noted, his knowl-

[5] This paragraph describing Llull's studies and achievement in Paris is omitted from the biography dictated by the saint himself. It seems likely that this omission was an intentional act of humility on his part, given his extraordinary and well-known success as a scholar and author. The account which is inserted here is based on the later biography written by Charles de Bovelles. The listing of Llull's writings which follows has been greatly abridged and is given only as a representative sample. The complete catalogue given by Charles de Bovelles contains well over a hundred works, some of which are no longer in existence. Yet, even this catalogue is far from complete and mentions only those works which had come to his attention. A more comprehensive listing of Llull's writings contains over three hundred titles, most of which are of considerable length.

edge of Latin grammar was rudimentary, he was not ashamed (although now forty years old) to attend basic classes in the company of mere youths. Such was his motivation and the brilliance of the divine illumination which he received that he soon attained an unrivaled mastery of Latin, the language of the Catholic Church and of scholarship.

Over the course of Ramon's life, inspired by the Holy Spirit, he composed innumerable books and treatises, in which his incomparable erudition is wonderfully manifested. The following are those titles which have come to my attention:

- *A Book for the Conversion of the Unbelievers*
- *The Book of Contemplation*
- *The Art of the Ten Propositions*
- *The Shorter Art*
- *On Miracles*
- *The Book of the Blessed Mary*
- *The Book of the Angels*
- *The Antichrist*
- *The Book of the Friend and the Beloved*
- *The Loving Art*
- *The Philosophy of Love*

- *A New Logic*
- *The Book of the Third Figure*
- *On Hell and the Underworld*
- *The Book of Beginnings*
- *The Tree of Knowledge*
- *The Art of Memory*
- *The Art of Medicine*
- *The Art of Law*
- *The Art of Navigation*
- *The Art of Astronomy*
- *On Preaching*
- *On Predestination*
- *The Dispute of Ramon and a Saracen*
- *The Book of Chaos*
- *The Book of Questions*
- *The Sixth Sense*
- *The Holy Land*
- *The Seven Sacraments*
- *The Five Wise Men*
- *The Experience of Reality*
- *The Mystical Art*
- *New Metaphysics*
- *The Infinite Being*
- *The Book of Physics*

- *The Form of God*
- *The Substance and Action of God*
- *The Book of Chemistry*

CHAPTER IV

Ramon returns to Majorca and learns Arabic from a servant, who comes to an unfortunate end.

AFTER A PERIOD of time engaged in scholarship in Paris, Ramon's family members and friends began to encourage him to return to his native land, the island of Majorca. Foremost amongst these well-intentioned and wise friends was [Saint] Raymond of Penyafort of the Order of Preachers. This was the same illustrious and holy Raymond whom Pope Gregory IX had entrusted with the compilation of his *Decretals* [a comprehensive collection of documents and decrees pertaining to canon law]. Ramon's relatives and friends pointed out to him that, if he intended to master Arabic, he could do so more readily in his home in Majorca, which is in far closer proximity to Africa than Paris is.

So, giving ear to the wise counsel of those who loved him, Ramon remained upon his native island of

Majorca. However, he no longer wore the fine clothing with which he had so vainly adorned himself previously and ceased to figure as a fashionable gallant in Majorcan society. Rather, he donned the simple habit of a Franciscan tertiary and lived a life of solitude, prayer, study, and austerity. Remaining firmly committed to his plan to evangelize the Saracens, he engaged an Arab as a servant, who instructed him in his native language. Ramon was a diligent, motivated, and gifted student and dedicated himself to mastering all the intricacies and subtleties of that difficult tongue.

But it happened that this Arab servant began to perceive how fervent and zealous his master was in the cause of converting his fellow Muslims. Fearing that he might succeed in this endeavor, the servant (who remained firmly committed to the creed of Mahomed) began to plot to murder Ramon. So, one day he attacked him, thrusting his dagger into his unwary master's chest. Fortunately, the wound, though serious, did not prove fatal. Ramon managed to seize the weapon from the hand of his servant and so escaped alive.

When his friends and relatives heard of this incident, they were enraged and wished to have the Arab servant put to death. Ramon himself, however, implored mercy for his assailant and erstwhile instructor. Thanks to his pleading for clemency, the Arab was spared the punishment of death and was sentenced to imprisonment instead. Alas, it happened that just a few days later, the servant, overcome by sorrow and despair, hung himself within his dungeon cell.[6]

---

6 This particular event is narrated more clearly and in a more edifying manner in the biography written by Charles de Bovelles. This version has been followed here.

CHAPTER V

Ramon lives as a hermit on Mount Rando and through divine inspiration, composes there his masterpiece, *The Greater Art*. An angel appears to him in the form of a shepherd and predicts wonderful things for his future endeavors.

After this had come to pass, Ramon then betook himself to a certain mountain, known as Mount Rando, not far from his home in Majorca. He climbed the mountain to its highest peak and there devoted himself to the contemplation of God in tranquility and solitude. He remained thus for some eight days and eight nights.

After this, as he stood still with his eyes gazing into the distant heavens, he received a sudden illumination from God. This illumination or revelation directed him to begin producing the great and magnificent book, the idea for which had come to him earlier.[7] This was

7 See page 12.

to be a book like no other, whereby he would be able to refute all the errors of the infidels and lead them to the splendor of the Truth. In this revelation, he was shown and instructed in all the details of the mysterious form and secret method whereby this momentous literary work was to be created. The saint[8] poured out effusions of prayers of deep gratitude to the Most High, who had deigned to select him for this honorable work and to give him the privilege of being its author.

Immediately after this, Ramon descended from the mountain and returned to his lodgings in the royal palace of the king of Majorca. He industriously started work on his great book, calling it at first *The Greater Art*, but later giving it the alternative title of *The General Art.* As part of this encyclopedic production, he wrote many smaller books, or chapters, which would together constitute the whole. In these, he laid down the specific and general principles of all fields of knowledge, thereby creating a universal key to all learning. This was done in such a manner that even the most simple-minded would be able to understand and thereby

---

[8] Ramon did not, of course, consider himself to be a saint, but this description (literally meaning "holy man") has been used by the scribe.

acquire mastery over the most abstruse and varied areas of studies.

Once he had completed writing this book in accordance with the instructions he had received from God, Ramon returned to the mountain. At the very spot where he had received his divine revelation, he constructed for himself a small hermitage, or hut. Dwelling there for more than four months, day and night he would pray to God. He earnestly begged the Lord, who had directed him to write *The Greater Art* for His honor and that of the Holy Catholic Church, to direct it mercifully to great success.

While Ramon was dwelling in this small mountain hermitage, engrossed in prayer as was his custom, a certain shepherd came upon him. This shepherd was youthful, with a friendly and pleasant face. He spoke to Ramon, telling him about the wonders and marvels of God, the heavens, and the angels. In the space of a mere hour, he communicated to the saint more than any other human being could have managed to say in the space of two entire days. The shepherd then noticed the volumes of the book, *The Greater Art*, that Ramon had written and which he had with him. Falling to his knees, he kissed them reverently, with tears of joy flowing from his eyes. He said to Ramon that through these volumes, a multitude of blessings would come to the Church of Christ.

The unknown shepherd then blessed Ramon and spoke of great things to come, just like one of the prophets of old. The shepherd then signed [Ramon's] head and his whole body with the Sign of the Holy Cross and departed.

Ramon was left marveling at what had transpired. Neither he nor anybody else had ever seen this mysterious shepherd before, nor did anyone ever see him again, and not a single person could say anything about who he was or whence he came.

CHAPTER VI

The king of Majorca encourages Ramon in his plan to establish a monastery for the instruction of future missionaries in foreign languages.

After this, the king of Majorca soon received news that Ramon had produced his marvelous book, *The Greater Art*. At once, he sent forth an order that Ramon should come to Montpellier [in France, near the Mediterranean coast], where he was then residing. When he arrived at the royal residence in Montpellier, Ramon was carefully questioned by a certain Franciscan friar appointed by the king for this purpose. In particular, the friar made enquiries about Ramon's *Book of Devotions*, which contained pious meditations for each and every day of the year. He was amazed to discover within these devotional paragraphs such an abundant richness of philosophy and Catholic doctrine.

Following this, Ramon composed another book, entitled *The Demonstrative Art*, in which he explained the principles of his masterpiece, *The Greater Art.* This new work he read publicly and lectured upon. He explained how the primal Chaos was a kind of form or element, upon which five attributes and ten predicates had been impressed by God to create each thing. Moreover, he demonstrated the consistency of this scheme with sound reason and universal and theological Truth.

At the time, Ramon also advanced a request to the king of Majorca. He asked him to construct a special training monastery in his kingdom and to provide it with the necessary funding and resources. It was Ramon's proposal that three suitably qualified friars of the Franciscan Order should be appointed to serve as professors there, instructing in the Arabic language men who would serve as future missionaries to the Muslims. He requested that the king pledge to pay five hundred florins a year to the monastery to ensure its ongoing operation.

After this, Ramon then went to Rome with the intention of advancing to the pope and the college of cardinals the proposal of establishing language schools for future missionaries throughout the world. But, alas, Pope Honorius IV had recently passed away, so the pontifical see was then vacant. Realizing that it was impossible to make his proposal at that time, Ramon left Rome and went to Paris, eager to promote to the world his new book, *The Greater Art*, which God Himself had directed him to write.

CHAPTER VII

Ramon returns to Paris and then visits Rome and other places. He tries, but fails, to obtain the support of the Papal Curia for the establishment of his monastery for the training of missionaries.

RAMON ARRIVED IN Paris during the time when Berthold was chancellor of the illustrious university of that city.[9] There, he read in a public lecture hall his commentary on his *Greater Art* at the special request of the aforesaid chancellor. This lecture was heard by the scholastics of that city, who read and considered his commentary with great attention but little understanding or appreciation.[10]

[9] This Berthold was appointed as chancellor of the University of Paris in 1288.

[10] This seems to be implicit in the next paragraph, in which Ramon moved to simplify his system "out of consideration for the weakness of the human intellect which he had witnessed in Paris."

Next, he returned to Montpellier, and there applied himself once more to lecturing and writing, producing a book entitled *The Art of Discovering the Truth.* He included in this volume, and in all the others he henceforth wrote, only four symbolic figures in his system of mastering knowledge. In his earlier *Greater Art,* he had used sixteen such figures. Now, out of consideration for the weakness of the human intellect which he had witnessed in Paris, he had reduced these figures by twelve, or rather, he had incorporated the principles of the twelve within the four new figures. This simplified his system of universal knowledge and made it easier to remember and apply.

Having satisfactorily achieved everything he set out to accomplish in Montpellier, he went forth next to the city of Genoa. Staying there only briefly, he translated the aforementioned new book, *The Art of Discovering the Truth,* into the Arabic language. Once this feat was completed, he directed his steps once more to the Roman Curia, eager to promote his campaign (as we have mentioned earlier) for the establishment of monasteries throughout the world, specially set up to train future missionaries in foreign languages.

But numerous obstacles and difficulties emerged in trying to gain the support of the Roman Curia for this plan. The saint realized that he would not be able to achieve much of what he intended in Rome at this point in time, and he resigned himself to this disappointing reality.

CHAPTER VIII

Ramon sets out for Africa but is overcome by fear of death while on the sea voyage. He returns to Genoa and is struck down by fever and despair.

RAMON REFLECTED DEEPLY on his lack of success in Rome in gaining support for his plan to establish language colleges for missionaries to the Muslims. He gave careful consideration to his situation and what he should do next. He resolved to return to Genoa and from thence to depart as a missionary to the land of the Saracens. He was eager to see whether he, single-handedly, could hold discussions with the wise men and scholars of the Muslim faith and prove to them, using the *Great Art* which God had given to him, the Truths of the Christian religion—namely, the incarnation of the Son of God and the highest unity of essence of the Divine Persons in the Most Blessed Trinity. For he knew that the Saracens did not believe such things themselves, but rather, like those who fail to see, they assert that we Christians actually believe in three deities.

News of the saint's plan became known in Genoa, and it soon became the talk of the town that Ramon was intending to cross the seas and enter the territories of the Arabs to convert them to faith in Christ. The citizens were greatly encouraged and edified by this heroic intention, and they hoped sincerely that God would perform marvelous works through this intrepid missionary. They also heard the story of Ramon's conversion experience and how he had received the plan of his great work by divine inspiration to bring about the conversion of the unbelievers.

Thus it was that the Lord visited Ramon through the rejoicing and support of the people of Genoa and shone upon him with all the radiance of the dawning sun. Nevertheless, at the same time, God began to give him the opportunity of proving the reality of his strength and faith in the face of adversity. For Ramon began to experience a very great trial. After he had made ready a ship for himself to cross the waters and loaded it with copies of his books and all the other materials he would need for his mission, he was assailed with terrible fears. Although he had been determined to undertake this missionary expedition with a firm resolve of mind, he know began to be plagued by its perils. What if the Saracens seize him as soon as he landed and slaughtered him? This seemed to be not unlikely. Or, if they did not do that, would they not incarcerate him in some dismal dungeon for the rest of his mortal days? Such thoughts loomed in his mind like gloomy and terrifying specters.

Therefore, Ramon, fearing for his skin (just as Saint Peter had once done during the passion of Our Lord), abandoned the resolution and plans which he had made, whereby he had committed himself even to die for Christ for the sake of converting the infidels to the Truth. And so, he remained in Genoa, prevented from his action by his own fear and left to himself. This happened by the dispensation and permission of the Lord, perhaps so that he would not become proud, and presumptive, and carried away by vain self-assurance.

So Ramon's ship departed, but without him on board. When the citizens of Genoa heard of this, they were scandalized and disappointed, for they had come to expect very great things of the would-be missionary. Ramon's heart was touched with deep sorrow at their disappointment, and he was no less disappointed in himself. He feared even that he would be eternally condemned by God because of his cowardice and vacillation. And although he was afflicted with such great melancholy and discouragement, he revealed the cause of his pain to no-one. Finally, in his weakened state, he succumbed to a severe fever and became very gravely ill, reduced almost to the point of death.

CHAPTER IX

Ramon experiences various visions in Genoa and considers joining the Dominicans. But he remains firm in his resolve to carry out missionary work for the glory of God, regardless of the dire spiritual trials he undergoes.

Translator's note: *This chapter is omitted from certain editions of Llull's memoirs (including the* Acta Sanctorum*), and its authenticity is not absolutely certain. The translation here is based on the text of the 1721 Mainz edition of Llull's* Opera Omnia. *It recounts somewhat disturbing visions and spiritual trials which the saint experiences in Genoa. At the time, he was still suffering from a severe fever, which may have contributed to this. Most contemporary scholars consider it to be genuine, and it certainly does not bear the marks of being a hagiographical legend.*

When the feast day of Holy Pentecost arrived, Ramon had himself carried to the church of the Dominicans [in Genoa]. When he heard the friars chanting the great hymn of that feast, *Veni Creator Spiritus*, he wept to himself, crying out in his heart: "Is not this Holy Spirit able to save even me?" [Overcome with anxiety and grief,] he was led, or carried, to the dormitory of the friars, where he threw himself down upon a bed for a while.

Then, gazing upwards, he perceived a small light at the very top of the chamber, glimmering like a pale star. And he heard a voice from where the star was situated, saying to him: "You can be saved only in this Order of St. Dominic!" Immediately, Ramon summoned some of the friars of the house to his presence and earnestly requested that he should be clothed in the habit of the Order of Preachers.[11] But the brethren were not able to comply with his wishes, as the superior of the house was absent at the time.

And so, Ramon returned to his home. A little later, he reflected and recalled to his memory how the Franciscan friars had received the work which the Lord had revealed to him on Mount Rando, *The Greater Art*, with much more readiness and enthusiasm than the

---

[11] This would clearly be as a Dominican tertiary rather than a fully professed friar.

Dominicans. Hence, he considered that the Franciscans would make more productive use of his *Art* for the honor of Our Lord Jesus Christ and the benefit of His Church. So, he pondered about whether, rather than becoming a Dominican, he should enter instead the Order of the Friars Minor of St. Francis.[12]

While he was weighing this up in his mind, there suddenly appeared to him a vision of a cincture or rope belt hanging from the wall close to him, such as is worn by the Franciscan friars. He was consoled by this vision, which seemed to confirm the directions his thoughts were taking. But then, after barely an hour, the same small light, resembling a pale star, which he had seen while lying in bed in the Dominican friary, appeared to him! And he heard a voice come from this light, which spoke as if giving him a command. "Did I not say to you," it said, "that you are able to be saved only in the Dominican Order? Take care, therefore, of what you do!"

Upon hearing this, Ramon was plunged into deep anxiety. According to this voice, he would be damned unless he entered the Dominicans. Yet, unless he chose

---

[12] Ramon was already a Franciscan tertiary at this point.

to remain with the Franciscans, his writings and methods which had been revealed to him by God would all come to nothing. When considering the question in this way, he was inclined to choose personal damnation for himself rather than the loss of his great work. For he knew that this work would bring about the salvation of a great multitude of souls and great glory and honor to God. To achieve it, he was ready to suffer anything, even the eternal perdition of his own immortal soul. So, disregarding the dire warning of the voice he had heard coming from the vision of the pale star, he summoned the superior of the local Franciscans to himself. And he promised to this superior that he would give himself completely to their order when he was closer to death.

Ramon, having surrendered his hope that God would lead him to final salvation, decided to make a formal declaration of his faith and a testament, lest the friars or the people should conclude that he was a heretic. [When he had done this, and] the priest offered to him the sacred Body of Christ, he sensed an invisible hand grab his face and twist it violently toward his right shoulder. He saw also the Eucharistic Host moving to his opposite shoulder and seemed to hear it say: "If you receive me now, you will suffer fitting punishment!"[13]

But, despite this frightening warning, Ramon remained firm in his resolve to suffer personal punishment rather than to give up the work of leading others to salvation. At that point, he again felt an invisible hand turning his head to the right but now perceived that the Body of Christ was at his right side too. Falling on his knees, he kissed the hand of the priest and received the Most Blessed Sacrament with the utmost devotion.

What an astonishing temptation—or rather, what an amazing testing of Ramon's resolve by divine providence! Just as the patriarch Abraham had believed and held firm in the face of testing and hoped against all hope, so did Ramon hold fast to the mission and method entrusted to him by God that would lead to the conversion of many and cause them to love and worship the Lord. And he did this even when it seemed to be at the price of his own salvation.

---

[13] This utterance was evidently not a divine pronouncement at all but perhaps an auditory hallucination caused by fever or anxiety, or possibly of demonic origin. It is possible that God may have *permitted* it to occur (without causing it) for the sake of testing Ramon's willingness to sacrifice himself for the glory of God.

In this trial, he was truly like the sun when it is obscured by a cloud. For it continues to shine brightly and burn ardently, despite the fact that it is completely covered with darkness. When Ramon was led into a state of similar spiritual darkness, despairing even of his own eternal salvation, he showed himself to love God, and to love his neighbor for the sake of God, infinitely more than he loved himself, as can be witnessed in the events recounted here.

CHAPTER X

Through prayer and the grace of God, Ramon recovers his spirits and resolution and sets forth for Tunisia.

[After the experience described in the previous chapter,] Ramon continued to lay in his sickbed in Genoa, held there both by grave illness of the body and heavy affliction of the soul. But during those days, a rumor was conveyed to him—that a certain galley was docked in the port in preparation for a voyage to Tunisia. When he heard of this, it was as if he was suddenly awaked from an oppressive slumber. Throwing off his torpor, he rushed to the ship, along with his collection of wonderful writings, and obtained for himself a place on it as a passenger bound for Tunisia.

But his friends, having seen him apparently placed at the very threshold of death during his illness, were filled with concern and fear for his well-being. They betook themselves to the ship, and against his will, they seized him and forcibly removed him from it, believing (of course) that this was for his own good.

A good while later, though, another ship arrived in the port, which was likewise bound for the realm of the Saracens—namely, to the land of Tunisia. This was of a type which Genoese refer to as a barge. So, the would-be missionary again collected together all of his books as well as other things necessary for his expedition. Acting in defiance to the wishes and advice of his misguided but well-intentioned friends, he boarded the barge.

As the ship set out upon the waters, carrying Ramon together with all the sailors, his heart was filled with a mystical and exultant joy. He had thought, while he had been under the dark cloud of his recent illness and depression, that this spiritual delight and enthusiasm had left him forever. But now he knew that through the mercy of the Holy Spirit, it had been restored to him once more. And not only this, but his physical health, which was still not yet perfect, suddenly began to improve and increase. Much to the amazement of those who witnessed it, and indeed to himself, within a few days he was stronger, more energetic, and more fully alive in both body and mind that he had ever been before.

CHAPTER XI

In Tunisia, he disputes boldly on questions of faith with the Saracens and speaks convincingly about the Holy Trinity.

HAVING GIVEN ABUNDANT thanks to God for his astonishing recovery, not long afterwards his ship arrived at the port of Tunisia. Gratefully setting his feet on dry land after the voyage, he soon entered the city. Day by day, Ramon slowly made the acquaintance of various experts in the law of Mahomed. Entering into conversation with them, he displayed himself to be well-versed in the principles of the Christian Faith and listened with attention as they advanced the tenets of their own creed (namely, that of Mahomed). He told them that if he found the arguments and explanations they advanced to be stronger and more logical than his own, he would be quite ready to be converted to their faith.

As news of this highly intelligent visitor, who was honestly willing to listen to the tenets of Islam, spread throughout the land, more and more of the learned adherents of that creed would come to see him, eager to convince him. Nevertheless, Ramon was able to answer their arguments easily and to demonstrate the greater strength of the Christian doctrines. He declared:[14] "Surely, it befits every wise man to adhere to whichever faith attributes to the eternal the greatest goodness, power, glory, and perfection—and all other such divine qualities—with the greatest coherence and harmony, and to which all the wise men throughout the world have given credence.

"Such faith must be held more praiseworthy by God, which professes the greatest possible concord and harmony between God, who is the highest and first Cause, and His creation. This is what I have demonstrated to you by my propositions. Now, all you Saracens who adhere to the creed of Mahomed overlook that God necessarily performs acts which exhibit His divine attributes

[14] In the following discourse, a number of sentences have been restructured and paraphrased to clarify the sense and nature of Ramon's argument. The essence of this argument is that the various elements of the Christian Faith (including the Holy Trinity, the Incarnation, the Passion, and Resurrection) are consist with, and necessary to, a belief in a God who is supremely powerful, good, merciful, just, etc.

and dignities. These acts of God are part of His intrinsic nature and are therefore eternal. Without acts of goodness, justice, power, perfection (and so forth), these attributes cannot be truly said to exist at all, and if these acts are denied as being proper and inherent to God, then the Deity is reduced to idleness and inertia. The acts of the highest Good are productive of good and are to create or bring about that which is good. The acts of the supreme Greatness are productive of greatness and are to create or bring about that which is great. The same may be said of all the other attributes of God—including justice, mercy, love, power, and so forth.

"But, according to your creed, you reduce the works of God to those of wisdom and will only. In this way, you exclude the other divine attributes (justice, power, love, goodness, etc.) from the actions of God, or you reduce them to inert principles. By doing this, you create an inequality between the various attributes of God and an incongruency between God and His works. But in the Christian belief, we hold to a system in which the attributes and actions of God are entirely congruent and harmonious. And this perfect congruence of divine attributes and actions is exhibited in our belief in the one, perfectly simple divine essence, in which there exists a Trinity of persons—that is, the Father, the Son, and the Holy Spirit.

"With the assistance of God, I shall be able to demonstrate to you why this belief in the Holy Trinity is consistent with the various divine attributes (such as goodness, justice, power, wisdom, and so forth) which we both believe in. I will do this by means of a certain Art or system, which was revealed (as is believed) by God Himself to a certain Christian hermit not very long ago.[15] If you are prepared to take just a few days to converse with me, in a spirit of tranquility and calm, I will convince you.

"Moreover, I will be able to demonstrate to you by means of this same Art that the incarnation of the divine Son, whereby the Creator was united with His creation in the one person of Christ, is fully and rationally congruent with belief in God as the highest and first Cause. We Christians believe also in the most noble Passion of this same Son of God, Christ, which He endured in the humanity He had assumed through His

---

[15] This Christian hermit to which Ramon refers here is, of course, himself. He seems to choose to speak of himself in this way out of humility, as if he does not wish to assert that he has personally received a revelation from God.

own will and mercy, for the purpose of redeeming us from the sin of our first parents and making us participants in God's eternal glory. We believe that this participation in and enjoyment of the eternal glory of God is the ultimate purpose and final state for which the blessed God created human beings in the first place.

"By means of the aforementioned Art, I shall demonstrate irrefutably and clearly that all of these divine actions, in which we Christians believe, are consistent with, and necessary concomitants of, the various divine attributes—such as power, mercy, justice, and so forth—which both Christians and Muslims consider to be intrinsic to God's essence."

CHAPTER XII

The king of Tunisia, fearing the effects of Ramon's preaching, arrests him and sentences him to death. The sentence is commuted to exile, with orders that Ramon should be stoned to death if ever he returns to Tunisia.

AND THUS IT was that Ramon began to illuminate the minds of unbelievers and to demonstrate the wisdom and rationality of Christian doctrine to them. But it happened that a certain Saracen, who was a prominent and influential man, came to hear the missionary and perceived what his intention was—namely, the conversion of his countrymen to Christ. He implored the king of Tunisia to order Ramon's beheading without delay, for (as he asserted) this foreigner was not only planning on subverting the Saracen people but also had the boldness and audacity to question and challenge the creed of Mahomed.

The king did not immediately follow his advice but [had Ramon arrested and detained in prison, and] summoned a council to determine what he should do. The prominent man who had made the complaint, however, supported by various others, eventually succeeded in turning the king's will and convincing him that the execution of Ramon was advisable. But there were other men amongst the Saracens who were prudent, just, and learned. These urged the king to avoid the sin of an unjustified killing. They counseled the monarch that it would be dishonorable, and an ill-becoming thing, and a disgrace to himself if he should put such a man as Ramon to death. For, they pointed out that although he was attempted to convince others of the Truth of his own Christian Faith, nevertheless he was distinguished by goodness of nature and wisdom. Moreover, they observed, it was held to be a noble thing for a Muslim to travel to the land of the Christians in an attempt to demonstrate the truth of their own creed. Applying the principles of justice and equity, it would be wrong to treat a Christian who followed this same course as if he was a criminal or malefactor.

The heart of the king was swayed by these wise and well-considered words, and he reversed his decision to have Ramon decapitated. Nevertheless, in order to maintain peace within his court and kingdom, he commanded that he [Ramon] should be expelled from his own realm of Tunisia. So the saint was released from custody—but not without suffering numerous hardship, beatings, and insults while incarcerated.

He was taken by Saracen officers to a certain ship bound for Genoa and placed on board. The edict of the king was read to him, stating that if he should ever return to the Kingdom of Tunisian, he would be stoned to death. Ramon was well-nigh heartbroken at being compelled to leave and was oppressed by heavy sorrow. For he knew that he had influenced a great many learned and influential men in Tunisia to understand Christian doctrine and to perceive its Truth. Indeed, many had come to desire to be baptized and thus to enter into the full and perfect light of the Catholic Faith.

The man of God was being tormented by such stings of disappointment and regret as he waited in the ship, which was just about to depart from Tunisia. As Ramon saw it, tribulations and sorrows faced him on all sides. If he were to leave Tunisia, as he had been ordered and was being compelled to do, he would be abandoning a multitude of souls who were drawing very near to accepting the Christian Faith. He knew that if he left, they would quite likely fall back into the snares of eternal damnation. If, on the other hand, he were to flee from the ship and remain where he was, he knew that he would face the fury of the Saracens who had opposed him, and who were already prepared to put him to death.

But the fire of divine love burnt strongly within him, and he did not fear the perils of death if he would be able to bring about the salvation of souls. So, he secretly escaped from the ship on which he had been placed and stealthily crept on to another vessel which had entered the harbor. It was his hope that the ship he had boarded would take him to some place from which he could readily return to Tunisia, evading the brutality of his opponents and bringing to fulfillment the good work of evangelization and conversion which had already commenced.

Now it happened, while all this was taking place, that a "certain Christian" who bore a close resemblance to Ramon (who, in fact, was *exactly* the same as him in both appearance and manner) happened to arrive in Tunisia. He entered the city and was immediately perceived by the astonished Saracens—for naturally, they assumed it was Ramon! They seized him and were about to stone him in accordance with the royal edict. But this unknown Christian exclaimed: “Stop! I am not who you think I am. I am not this Ramon at all!”

So the Saracens investigated the matter and found that Ramon had indeed been placed upon the ship, and so the man whom they had arrested was set free and allowed to go about his business.

Thus it was that Ramon remained in Tunisia for a further three weeks. But he saw that he was not able to achieve the conversions that he had intended and that his work was not bearing fruit at that point. And so, he resolved to travel to Naples.

Translator's note: *There is an apparent narrative inconsistency here, if the text is taken in a strictly literal sense. Since it is stated that Ramon escaped from the ship on which he was placed and secretly boarded another, it is not clear how he then spends a further three weeks in Tunisia engaged in his missionary work. It seems probable that the mention of an “unknown Christian” who bears an exact resemblance to Ramon is in fact a literary device for referring to Ramon himself after he departed from the ship under the cloak of secrecy. A number of considerations support this theory.*

Firstly, it would account for how Ramon or his biographer came to be aware of this event, which otherwise seems to be inexplicable. Secondly, it is consistent with Ramon still being present in Tunisia and trying to continue his missionary work. The translation offered here is intended to highlight this interpretation of the unknown Christian as being a literary device for referring to Ramon himself, since now he would be clearly in hiding from the authorities and could not use his true identity openly.

CHAPTER XIII

Ramon travels to Naples and there teaches his *Greater Art*. He again seeks the support of the Papal Curia and the kings of Genoa and France for his missionary colleges but without success.

[AFTER RAMON HAD left Tunisia where he had been compelled to remain in hiding, he boarded a ship to Naples and arrived there in due course.] At Naples, he presented lectures on his *Art* and remained there until the election of a new pontiff, Pope Celestine V. After this, he visited the Roman Court once again and sought to obtain support for the plan which he had longed to carry out, for the sake of propagating the Christian Faith—namely, the establishment of monasteries or academies which could serve as training centers in foreign languages for future missionaries. While in Rome, he also applied himself to writing diligently, producing a number of new books during this time.

After a little time had passed, Pope Celestine V was succeeded in the pontificate by Pope Boniface VIII. Ramon saw the new pope and implored him with all his efforts to support this project of establishing missionary academies, which would be so useful for spreading the Christian Faith to the unbelieving peoples. Although the saint suffered much anguish and anxiety on account of his efforts in following the pope persistently in the pursuit of his goal, he did not cease from working for what he was determined to achieve. He hoped without any doubt that the pope would eventually deign to listen favorably to his request—for indeed, he knew that he was not simply asking for a personal favor for his own benefit but rather supplicating unceasingly for something which was for the good of the entire Catholic Church.

But, for various reasons, Ramon did not encounter any success. After persisting patiently and diligently, he was eventually compelled to resign himself to the fact that his request would not obtain support at this point in time. And so, in this spirit of holy resignation, he betook himself once more to the city of Genoa. Once back in that city, he applied himself to his literary and scholastic endeavours once more, producing several more books.

His next move was to seek an audience with the king of Majorca. This he did, and then he journeyed once more to Paris. In that great city, he delivered many lectures on his wonderful *Art* and composed a multitude of further books. He also arranged to speak to the king of France. He made to him the same request which he had recently advanced to the papal court regarding the establishment of academies or monasteries for the teaching of foreign languages to prepare men for missionary work to the Saracens.

But Ramon perceived once again that his request, though made for the benefit of the Holy Church of God, was making no or little impact. So, he returned once more to his homeland, the isle of Majorca. He remained there for a long while. Now, at that point in history, there were a considerable number of Saracens living in Majorca. Ramon made good use of his time by endeavoring to convert these Saracens to the true Faith through both preaching and disputation. He also authored yet a few more volumes while he was there.

CHAPTER XIV

Ramon journeys to Cyprus and works to convert the many schismatic and heterodox Christians and unbelievers there. He requests that the king of Cyprus should send him to the sultan and other Saracen monarchs, but his request is not granted.

IT HAPPENED THAT, as Ramon continued his scholarly labors at Genoa, a remarkable piece of news reached his ears. It was said that the emperor of the Mongols, Ghazan Khan,[16] had invaded Syria and annexed it to his own dominion.[17] As soon as Ramon heard this, he hastened to travel to the island of Cyprus. [For he

[16] In the Latin text, the term *Tartars* is used instead of Mongols, and the name given is Cassanus (a Latinized form of Ghazan.) There is evidence that Ghazan Kan (1271–1304) was actually baptized and raised as a Nestorian Christian and educated also in Buddhist doctrines but later converted to Islam.

[17] Ramon's views on the importance and relative ease of converting the Mongols to Christianity is outlined in the *Masterplan for the Conversion of Unbelievers*, included in this volume.

planned to go forth to Syria from there and take the opportunity of speaking to the Ghazan Khan in the hope of converting him to the Christian Faith.] But when he arrived at Cyprus, he discovered that the story he had heard was, in fact, false.

So, he carefully considered his present position. Now that he was in Cyprus, he was determined not to waste the time and opportunity that he had but to apply it to work that would be acceptable in the sight of God and beneficial to his fellow men. He recalled in his heart the words of the apostle St. Paul: "Let us cease not to do good; for, in due season, we shall reap a harvest as long as we do not cease from our efforts."[18] He considered also the words of the psalmist, which declare that: "They go forth sowing their seed in tears, and return in exultation carrying their harvest."[19]

Accordingly, Ramon arranged to meet with the king of Cyprus. With the greatest possible earnestness, he entreated the Cyprian monarch to permit him to preach to the multitude of heretical and schismatic Christians who dwelt on his island—including Monophysites[20]

---

[18] Gal. 6:9.

[19] Ps. 125:6.

[20] The Monophysites believe in the divinity and humanity of

and Nestorians[21]—as well as the many Muslim residents there also. Furthermore, he asked the king that, once he had preached to the local schismatics and infidels and done all he could for their edification, he should send him forth to the sultan, who was a Saracen, and to the kings of Egypt and Syria, so that he could teach them the Truth of the holy Catholic Faith. However, the king did not have the least interest in any of these things.

But Ramon was not to be discouraged so easily. Trusting in Him who evangelizes His word with great strength and virtue, and with God as his only helper, he began to work courageously among the heretics and infidels of Cyprus, using both disputation and preaching. But although he was strenuous in this undertaking and persisted unwaveringly, a sudden serious physical illness fell upon him, bringing him close to death once again.

Christ but believe He has a single nature, which is both divine and human. Catholics believe that Christ was a single person but with two natures—one divine and one human. The Monophysite position arose as a reaction to Nestorianism and Arianism. Coptic, Ethiopian, and Eritrean Orthodox Churches all belong to this group.

[21] Nestorian Christians believe in both the divinity and humanity of Christ, but conceive it in a way such that the unity of the person of Christ is not strongly maintained. The Syriac Churches of the East belong to this group.

CHAPTER XV

Ramon discovers that his two companions, one of whom is a cleric, have been poisoning him. He survives the attempt on his life and dismisses them both. He receives a favorable reception from the grand-master of the Order of the Temple, then continues to seek support for the establishment of missionary colleges.

Now, in those days, Ramon had two companions who acted as his assistants and attendants. One of these was a cleric[22] and the other a lay servant. These two, being unmindful that all they did was done in the sight of God and negligent of their own salvation, had plotted together to bring about the demise of the man of God and had been secretly administering poison to him. [This poisoning had been the cause of the unexpected illness which had befallen him.] When

[22] The term cleric here could refer to anyone in engaged in studies (or who had once been engaged in studies) in preparation for Holy Orders.

Ramon discovered their treachery and disloyalty, he was deeply grieved. But, with a merciful heart, he simply dismissed them from his service and took no further action against them.

Next, Ramon visited the city of Famogusta [in northern Cyprus]. Following this, he was received joyfully by the grand-master of the Order of the Knights Templar,[23] who resided in Limassol [in southern Cyprus].[24] He remained as a guest at the palace of the grand-master until he was restored to perfect health.

Once he was well again, Ramon sailed for the city of Genoa once more. While there, he applied himself to writing and produced a great many meritorious books. And then he went on to Paris. There, he delivered effective lectures on his *Art* for the benefit of the scholars and professors of the venerable university of that city. Moreover, he produced yet more writings.

During the pontificate of Pope Clement V, Ramon bade farewell to the city Paris and moved to Lyon [in

[23] This would have been Jacques de Molay, the twenty-third and final grand-master of the Templars. When the Templars were disbanded, he was incarcerated in Paris and would have been there when Ramon was dictating this memoir.

[24] At this stage, the city of Limassol was owned and governed by the Knights Templar, who had their headquarters there.

southern France, where the pope was temporarily residing]. The intrepid scholar made arrangements to have an audience with the Supreme Pontiff of the Church. There, he implored the pope to support his proposal, which would bring the greatest possible benefits for the Faith. He asked, as he had asked several times before, that the pope should establish monasteries or academies throughout Europe to which devout and suitable men could go to acquire knowledge of the languages of the various infidel nations. The graduates of these academies would be well-equipped to proclaim the Gospel as missionaries, in accordance with the precept of the Lord which instructs His disciples to "go forth into all the world, and preach the Gospel to every creature."[25]

But, alas, neither the pope nor even any of the cardinals had the slightest interest in Ramon's proposal.

---

[25] Mark 16:15.

CHAPTER XVI

Ramon travels to Algeria, where he preaches the Gospel fearlessly. He attracts the attention of the local imam and narrowly escapes death. He then departs but barely survives a shipwreck on the voyage back to Europe.

So Ramon, disappointed with his lack of success at the Papal Curia, decided once more to return to his native island, Majorca. From there, he sailed to the Saracen territory of Béjaïa [a port city in Algeria]. In this city, he stood up in the central square and boldly proclaimed in a loud voice to all the people there present: "The faith of the Christian is the true faith, holy and acceptable to God! The faith of the Muslims is false and erroneous! This I am prepared to prove to you." And after he made this declaration and urged the great crowds of unbelievers there present to faith in Christ, they rushed upon him furiously, intending to stone him to death.

News of this quickly reached the ears of the imam[26] of the city, who sent orders to the people to desist from the stoning of this stranger. Rather, he commanded that he should be brought into his own presence. This was done, and the imam questioned him thus: "Why is it, O wayfarer, that you are thus deceived, that you should, for the sake of the law of your Christ, impugn the law of our Mahomed? Surely you are not ignorant that whosoever shall do so must pay with his life?"

To this, Ramon replied without hesitation: "The true servant of Christ who knows the depths of the Catholic Faith should not fear the death of his own mortal body when he sees that he has a chance of attaining the eternal life of the spirit for the souls of all those who accept the true faith he proclaims."

The imam considered this before continuing: "If you consider the law of Christ to be true and the law of Mahomed to be false, please present your proofs for this contention." Now, this particular imam had a distinguished reputation as a philosopher and thinker. So Ramon began by asking him: "You believe that God is perfectly good, do you not?" The imam replied that

[26] The Latin text uses the term *episcopus* (literally, *bishop*) here.

it was indeed so. Then Ramon argued: "The perfect Good must be perfect within itself, and not needing any other good beyond itself. But if you deny the mystery of the Holy Trinity, then you are denying that God was the perfect Good from eternity.

"Goodness is greater when it pours itself forth and overflows itself to another. Now, if you reject the Trinity and believe that God only began to generate other goodness when the world was created, you are denying the perfect and absolute goodness of God—since, as noted, goodness is greater in its outpouring than its remaining inert. But the doctrine of the Trinity implies that God has *eternally* been outpouring and overflowing His goodness, insofar as the Son is eternally begotten and the Spirit proceeds eternally from both the Father and the Son. To sum up, the doctrine that God is the absolute and eternal goodness implies that God has always been pouring forth this goodness—in other words, that the greatest possible Good has been eternally giving rise to the greatest possible Good. And this is to be found in the Holy Trinity, of the eternal Begetter, the eternally Begotten, and the Spirit which proceeds eternally from both. Thus the doctrine of the

Trinity alone is consistent with the supreme and eternal goodness of God!"

When the imam heard this powerful and irrefutable argument, he was astonished and speechless. Unable to think of any word to utter in reply, he ordered that Ramon be placed in prison for the time being. Now a multitude of Saracens were gathered around outside the imam's palace, expecting to stone him once their spiritual leader had finished his interview with him. But the imam sent forth an edict that Ramon was not to be killed by the crowd, for, indeed, he intended to deal with him himself. So, the saint was taken off to prison, suffering much hardship and mistreatment at the hands of his guards—including being beaten by rods, being dragged along by his beard (which was then very long and full), and being confined for a time within the prison latrine, where his suffering was very great. After a while, however, he was taken to a regular cell in this same prison.

The next day after this had taken place, all the Muslim clerics in the area went as a group to the imam, requesting that Ramon should be put to death. But some discussion and disputation arose about the justice of such a sentence. Eventually, it was resolved that Ramon should be brought before the assembly of clerics and examined. If he was found to be intelligent and in his right mind [and therefore responsible for his actions and words], he would indeed be put to death. But if, on the contrary, he was found to be a mere babbling fool or insane, his life would, in mercy, be spared.

Now there happened to be among the assembly of Muslim clerics one who had heard Ramon previously when he was in Tunisia. He said: "I strongly advise you against giving this man a hearing at all. For I have heard him myself often. He is very clever, and I know from experience that he will say things against the law of Mahomed to which no good reply can be formulated!" So, after further discussion, it was agreed not to summon Ramon before the assembly at all but to confine him in a harsher place of incarceration than where he was currently being detained.

But there were also in the assembly of Muslim clerics certain men who had spent time in Majorca or Genoa. They knew of Ramon's reputation for wisdom and his goodness. So, in a spirit of justice and decency, they argued that it was befitting that such a distinguished scholar should be detained in more comfortable dwellings. And this view was accepted by the majority of the council and agreed to by the imam himself. And so it was done.

For about six months, Ramon remained in detention in the accommodation which had been arranged for him. Very often, Saracen clerics would visit, and even messengers from the imam. They would try to convince him to accept the law of Mahomed, both by argument and also by bribes and other inducements. For he was assured that if he accepted their faith, he would be granted brides, public honors, and considerable wealth. But, founded upon the firm rock of God, Ramon responded to such offers by saying: "I, on my part, make to you this counteroffer—if *you* are willing to believe in the Lord Jesus Christ and to renounce your own erroneous law, then I shall grant to you eternal and infinite riches in the world to come and will promise to you unending life in paradise!"

Since Ramon and the Muslim clerics who visited him very frequently reached a deadlock in their theological and philosophical disputes, it was eventually agreed that each side should write a single book. Each party—both the Muslim scholars and Ramon, who represented Christianity—would compile the very best arguments and lines of reasoning they could find or formulate to support their respective creeds. And they agreed that whoever produced the most convincing book would be considered to have the right religion.

But, as Ramon was still laboring to produce the very best book possible, the king of Béjaïa, who then resided in the city of Constantine,[27] sent forth a decree that the missionary philosopher was to be expelled immediately from his kingdom.

In accordance with this, Ramon was placed aboard a ship, and the captain of the ship was instructed that, pursuant to the decree of the king, the prisoner should not be permitted to set foot on Algerian soil again. Now, the ship happened to be traveling to Pisa. When it was about ten miles away from the port of Pisa, a violent tempest suddenly arose. The vessel was tossed about by powerful gales in every direction and eventually torn apart by the ferocity of the storm.

Many of those on board were killed and sank into the depths of a watery grave. But, miraculous as it may seem, Ramon, together with his servant, managed to survive. Though he lost many of his precious books and much of his clothing, he and his servant clung to a small raft and eventually arrived safely on Italian shores.

---

[27] A city in Eastern Algeria.

CHAPTER XVII

Ramon arrives in Naples, where he begins an ambitious campaign for the unification of the Catholic military orders and a new crusade. He continues to travel through Europe, and while in Paris, refutes the errors of Averroes.

SHORTLY AFTERWARDS, HE entered the city of Pisa. Certain citizens there received him very honorably. The man of God was, by this stage, elderly and somewhat frail. Nevertheless, he did not cease to labor tirelessly for the sake of Christ, and brought his *Ultimate General Art*, which he had been working upon and revising throughout most of his life, to its final and most perfect form. The immense efficacy of this *Art*, as well as other books of Ramon, is worthy of the very highest recognition. For, these works are all intended not for the passing glory of this world or for the adulation of vain and empty philosophy but rather for establishing strong love of God and wisdom in divine Truths. In this way, they aspire to the highest and most noble Good.

Once Ramon had completed this *Ultimate General Art* to his satisfaction, and also penned innumerable other books there, he turned his attention to encouraging the citizens of Pisa to the service of Christ. He therefore addressed the council of the city and extolled to them the merits of establishing an order of Christian soldiers for the purpose of recovering the Holy Land. This new military order of Christian knights would, he proposed, wage tireless war against the multitude of unbelievers who had taken possession of the land were Christ had once trod.

The municipal council of Pisa were deeply moved by Ramon's eloquence and wisdom in encouraging them to this endeavor. Accordingly, they wrote a formal letter addressed to the pope and the court of cardinals outlining this plan and asking for permission and support. They entrusted this letter to the man of God to present to His Holiness when he had the opportunity.

Departing from Pisa, Ramon then made his way to Genoa once more. Addressing the council of that city in a similar manner, he obtained letters of support for his plan from them also. What was more, many devout matrons, holy widows, and other members of the nobility pledged to donate 30,000 florins in support of this new order of knights and their future military campaign.

Once more, the business was entrusted to the saint. He then made his way to the papal court in Avignon, for the pope was residing there at this point.[28] But once again, Ramon met with no success in the worthy cause he was seeking to advance.

Resigning himself to this state of affairs, the man of God again headed to Paris. There he presented many lectures on his *Art*, with a great multitude of professors and scholars attending. He carefully demonstrated to them how his method could establish any form of truth in a marvelous manner, whether it was the truths of the physical sciences or the veracity of the doctrines of the Catholic Faith. He also applied himself to writing and produced a large number of further books.

Ramon observed, however, that many academics in Paris were departing or swerving away from the orthodox teachings of the Church. This was primarily because of the influence of certain commentaries on

---

[28] From 1309 to 1376, a series of seven popes resided at Avignon, in France, beginning with Pope Clement V, who is also the first French pope.

Aristotle which were then in circulation, specifically those of the Muslim philosopher Averroes.[29] Some of these scholars even went so far as to say that the doctrines of the Catholic Faith, so far as they could be understood or expressed, were logically impossible. Nevertheless, they opined also that the doctrines of the Catholic Faith were true, insofar as they were to be believed by the Christian faithful.

Ramon applied himself to refuting this position, demonstrating that the doctrines of the Catholic Faith, were, in fact, comprehensible to and consistent with reason. For, he said, anything which was found to be impossible to the person who understood it could not also be held to be true by the same person—because the same proposition cannot be simultaneously true and impossible, nor could something which is held to be incomprehensible also be held to be true. He produced several treatises propounding this position in opposition to the errors of Averroes.

---

[29] Averroes was a twelfth-century Muslim scholar and philosopher from Andalusia in Spain who wrote on philosophy, medicine, astronomy, and mathematics. He wrote commentaries on Aristotle, which were translated into Latin and became influential in the West.

The saint heard that the Holy Father, Pope Clement V, was in Vienne[30] for the purpose of celebrating a general council. This Council of Vienne was to be convened in the Year of Our Lord 1311 on the first day of October. Ramon resolved to be present at this council and to advance there three proposals, or requests, for the strengthening and reparation of the true Faith.[31]

First, he asked that suitable colleges be established where devout and intelligent men could be trained in the various languages of the non-Christian peoples to equip them to go forth in a spirit of charity to preach the doctrine of the Gospel to foreign lands. Second, he proposed that the various Catholic military orders

---

30 A city in southeast France.

31 The proposals made by Ramon at this time are documented and explained in the *Libellus de Fine* (*Booklet on the Goal*), which he wrote at this time, addressing the work to Pope Clement V. Substantial extracts from this book are included in this volume (as his *Masterplan for the Conversion of the Unbelievers*), providing details of his plans for the establishment of missionary colleges. The same booklet also includes his proposal for a new order of Christian knights to fight a crusade to reclaim the Holy Land and strategies for waging the crusade. Since these memoirs were dictated by Llull in September 1311, he must have traveled to Vienne before the commencement of the council (in October 1311) to make his proposals and requests to the pope.

should be formed into a single new order of Christian knights, which would be sufficiently large and strong to recover possession of the Holy Land from the Saracens. Third, he requested that the pope should act immediately to eliminate the growing influence of Averroes and his perverse errors within the academic world. He proposed that this could be done by sending forth learned and orthodox men intent not upon their own glory but on the honor of Christ to refute those misguided doctrines which were contrary to the uncreated Truth and Wisdom.

Upon this topic, Ramon compiled a small book entitled *The Book of the Birth of Jesus Christ as a Small Infant*. In this booklet, he promises to refute the view of Averroes and his followers using the principles of both science and of theology. And this he did in brilliant fashion in some of his other volumes.

CHAPTER XVIII

A summary of Ramon's career thus far.

RAMON, THE SERVANT of God, who endeavored to communicate the highest and most profound Truth of the Trinity, produced, amidst his daily labors, more than 123 books![32]

At this stage, forty years had elapsed since he first offered his whole heart and soul and all his strength and of all his mind to God. During this time, he had continually and diligently brought forth writings whenever he had the leisure to do so. For this reason, he deservedly was able to pronounce the words of the prophet David when he said: "My heart has brought forth a good word. I will therefore declare my work to

[32] This estimate, while impressive, falls far short of Llull's complete literary output. A comprehensive catalogue of his writings includes well over three hundred titles. Most of these works are of considerable length.

the King, my tongue like the pen of a scribe."[33] Truly indeed was the tongue of Ramon like the hand of that uncreated and invisible Scribe—namely, the Holy Spirit, who gives the divine word in great strength to those who proclaim the Gospel. Of the work of the Spirit, our Savior Himself said to His apostles: "It is not you who shall speak, but the Spirit of your Father which will speak in you."[34]

Animated by a wish for his books to be accessible and useful to all peoples, he translated many of them into the Arabic language that he had taken pains to master. These books have spread throughout the entire world. But there are three principal centers where they are gathered and preserved: in a Carthusian monastery in Paris, with a certain nobleman in the city of Genoa, and with another nobleman in Majorca.

Translator's note: *At this point, the memoir of Ramon Lull reaches its end. This memoir was dictated in September 1311 in Paris to an unknown scribe, who compiled the saint's recollections into the account offered above.*

---

33 Ps. 44:1.

34 Matt. 10:20.

Clearly, certain comments and observations have been inserted by the scribe, such as the praises of Llull's writing and comments about his sanctity, which he would hardly have made himself. The next and final chapter, in which his martyrdom is described, is taken from another reliable biography written by Charles de Bovelles in the early sixteenth century.

CHAPTER XIX

Ramon returns to Tunisia, an old man but still vigorous and strong. He preaches the Gospel there once more and is stoned to death. The next night, some merchants from Majorca see a pyramid of brilliant light coming from where his body is lying. They collect his remains and return them reverently to Majorca.

Translator's note: *This final short chapter is not from the memoir dictated by Llull himself, which (for obvious reasons) does not include an account of his final days and martyrdom. Rather, it is taken from the biography of Ramon written by Charles de Bovelles, a celebrated French mathematician, philosopher, and theologian of the fifteenth and sixteenth centuries. For the sake of continuity, the beginning of the chapter begins from the same point at which the memoir dictated by the saint concludes.*

So it was that in all his labors and plans for the advancement of the Catholic Faith, Ramon never succeeded in obtaining support from any pope or king.

Nevertheless, he persisted indefatigably in his efforts, always determined and courageous in the face of hardships. Many were his days of toil and sleepless nights, as he undertook perilous missionary journeys and wrote countless books. In all of this, he offered his entire soul to the Lord without reserve.

As we have said, his writings can scarcely be numbered. They were written in three main languages—Latin, Spanish, and Arabic (for the sake of the Saracens). As mentioned earlier, this difficult language he mastered through a Saracen servant of his. His manuscripts are now held with the Carthusians in Paris, with whom he frequently stayed as a guest; at Genoa, with a certain nobleman who supported his work; and with another nobleman on the island of Majorca, who again frequently accommodated him as a guest.

By now, Ramon was drawing close to the end of his life. In the body, he was an old man. But in his soul, he remained vigorous, and drawing from this strength of soul, he found an inexhaustible resource of energy. He left once more for Tunisia to renew his missionary work there, departing from Majorca.

When he arrived, he was recognized immediately by the local inhabitants, who recalled that he had been expelled from their country, under pain of death, many years earlier. Without mercy, he was stoned to death, and his dead body left near the port of the city, covered in the rocks which had killed him.

The next night, according to the will of God, certain merchants from Majorca happened to arrive by ship in the port of Tunisia. From a distance, they perceived an immense pyramid of light shining brilliantly into the night sky. Tracing its source, they discovered that this mysterious and radiant light originated from a pile of rocks, which they found by the port.

Filled with astonishment, they investigated by removing the stones to discover the lifeless body of the man of God underneath. Immediately, they recognized him as their learned and devout compatriot, Ramon Llull. Quickly, they placed his mortal remains upon the ship and returned them to the island of Majorca. There, they were fittingly and reverently buried. And there, his body remains to this very day, with a multitude of miracles occurring at the sight of his tomb.

The teachings of this man of God are filled with living and lifegiving doctrine. This is not my opinion only but is the judgement of many other learned men. For whoever reads his work diligently will sense it to be the fruit not merely of human intelligence but rather filled with celestial wisdom. It is indeed as if the wisdom of the Holy Spirit perfected Ramon's human intelligence and worked through it whenever mere mortal capacities had reached their limit. Thus, he arrived at insights which no amount of human toil or time could ever suffice to produce.

All the deeds and marvels which have been recounted in this narrative of Ramon's life and death, of which we have given witness, suffice to show that he was most truly one of the saints and is now a blessed citizen of the Kingdom of God; to whom be glory and honor forever and ever. Amen.

BLESSED RAMON LLULL'S MASTERPLAN FOR THE CONVERSION OF UNBELIEVERS AND THE RECLAIMING OF THE HOLY LAND

Addressed to Pope Clement V

Translator's note: *The following are extracts from Ramon Llull's* Libellus de Fine (Small Book about the End),[35] *which was apparently written when he advanced a number of proposals for the consideration of the pope and cardinals just before the Council of Vienne in 1311. The texts given below are taken from the edition published in Palma, Majorca, in 1665. As becomes clear at various points in the text, the work is often specifically addressed to the pope. This would have been Pope Clement V (the first of the so-called Avignon popes).*

---

[35] This could also be translated as *Small Book about the Goal/Purpose.* The title seems to imply both senses.

Author's Prologue

OUR GOD AND LORD, JESUS CHRIST: May this humble work, entitled, *The Book about the End,* be to Your praise, reverence, and honor!

The world is now in a deplorable state, and still it is to be feared that it may slip into a worse one. The number of Christians inhabiting the globe is relatively few, but the number of infidels of various kinds is vast. Many of these strive each day to overthrow the Christians by conquering Christian territories and annexing them to their own dominions. As part of this campaign of conquest, they deny the mysteries of the Most Holy Trinity and the Incarnation of Our Lord Jesus Christ. And, to the great dishonor of the celestial court, they have now seized control of the Holy Land.

And yet, there are many Christians who remain reluctant to provide any remedy to this regrettable state of affairs. But there is at least one individual of whom I know[36] who has made it his life's work, traveling long

[36] Ramon is here referring to himself but does so, by means of this circumlocutionary mode of expression, for the sake of humility.

and far, to secure support for this cause from His Holiness the pope, the college of cardinals of the Roman Church, and with many other Catholic sovereigns and princes. Accordingly, I propose that His Holiness the pope, the lord cardinals, and other princes should act to establish monasteries in which literate men, willing to suffer even death for the sake of Christ, could learn the diverse languages of the unbelievers. By this means, they could go forth to proclaim the Gospel to the entire world in accordance with the precept of Our Lord Jesus Christ, who said to Saint Peter: "Peter, if you love Me, feed My sheep."[37]

But, alas, I have been able to achieve so far nothing of my endeavor to obtain support for this proposal. The good of humanity is apparently a cause which has no friends—or, if it does, they are very few! For in this present age, devotion and charity have been forgotten (as anyone who looks may see). And because I have already written a great many books against the errors of the infidels, the elevation of the human intellect, and the mastery of all fields of learning, I shall entitle this current work *The Book of the End.* In this work, I shall

[37] John 21:17.

hopefully exonerate myself before God the Father, His most just Son, and the Holy Spirit, who examines the human heart; as well as before the Most Blessed Virgin Mary, the Mother of the Incarnate Son of God, and the whole heavenly court of all the saints.

At this point, I am not able to do anything more than write this work, for I have found none to help me in my plans. I propose to send a copy of this book to the Lord Pope and other leaders of the Christian Faith. Through the grace of Jesus Christ, may it help to bring all peoples of the world to the one holy sheepfold of the Catholic Church!

Plans for the Establishment of a New Missionary Order and Colleges for the Training of Missionaries

A new religious order is needed whose goal it is to bring about the permanent conversion of the unbelieving nations to the Christian Faith. For this to happen, the pope and the college of cardinals must appoint a particular cardinal whose duty it is to administer this order, free of all other burdens of office. Four monastic houses should be established in suitable and amenable locations. These monasteries, or academies, would need to be provided with sufficient funding on an ongoing basis to teach languages to students and to obtain the books necessary for doing so.

The expenses of this would be quite modest, from the point of view of the total assets of the Church. There are many bishops and prelates, who, if they committed only a fifth part of their income, could quite easily fund such a monastery.

The lord cardinal who is appointed to govern this new order ought to have trustworthy assistants and cooperators who would be capable of selecting devout and literate men. These men, to be educated and formed as future missionaries, must be individuals who burn with an ardent desire to learn these foreign languages. They must be men who are willing to engage in great labor and hardship with the utmost charity and patience and even to die (if necessary) for our most merciful Lord, Jesus Christ, the Son of God. For He did not fear to lay down His own life for the salvation of others. Suitable men could be found both from the ranks of the religious and from the laity, and when they were found, be admitted (with the permission and authorization of the Supreme Pontiff) to one of these educational monasteries for training.

To me, it seems quite sufficient that in each of these institutions there should be twelve brethren, together with a superior. And as soon as each student had attained to proficiency in two languages, they could be sent forth on missions of evangelization to the lands of the unbelievers. Whenever this happened, two new students could be admitted to the monastery to take their places [. . .].

The Catholic Faith began through the preaching of the apostles and was then multiplied by sanctity, by the shedding of the blood of the martyrs, and by sheer hard work. Hence, it follows that its continued multiplication and expansion depends upon having missionaries of true sanctity who have the courage to face martyrdom and are ready for tireless toil. But why is it, one may ask, that we do not see such expansion today? It is because we no longer have men who are willing to face martyrdom for the Faith or preachers or laborers who are filled with such fervent desire as in times past. We no longer have people who possess the great sanctity which can come only from striving to be holy even as Our Lord and God is holy. Is it any wonder that today we no longer witness the miracles and progress of the Faith which abounded in the time of the apostles?

O Holy Father and Pope, how you shall be blessed! O my lord cardinals, how greatly you shall be rewarded by God! And, most of all, how blessed will be whichever holy cardinal shall undertake the leadership of this new missionary order. Begin this work, therefore; begin it now, for God!

For death comes to each of us quickly, and a thousand years have elapsed in which this urgent work of conversion has been neglected. Do not fear to speak out, and do not fear any lack of funds, as if some bishops or prelates will be unwilling to provide financial support for this good work for God!

Do you not know that the Saracens cultivate special flowers[38] for the sake of temporal goods of this world? Would it be any astonishing thing for *you* to cultivate and contribute to the training of holy men for the sake of multiplying the honors of Jesus Christ and for the salvation of the nations?

---

[38] The exact meaning of the word in the original text here, *arciscinus*, has not been determined, and it is not found in any standard or even specialist dictionaries. The word *narciscinus* is found in a medical work of the Muslim scholar Avicenna (d. 1037) (apparently a transliteration of an Arabic word), amongst a listing of the varieties of flowers whose oil can be used for medical purposes. This would seem to be consistent with its present context, although the precise type of flower referred to is uncertain.

I urge you to recall that when the apostles said to Jesus Christ, "We have two swords," He replied to them, "It is enough."[39] By this is signified that you ought to battle both by the work of preaching and by force of arms to overcome unbelief. Or do you not know that Christ said: "Whoever is not for me is against me"?[40] And He exhorted you to give your very all for His sake when He commanded us to "love the Lord your God with all your heart, with all your soul, with all you mind, and with all your strength."[41]

A Description of the Saracens and Strategies for Their Conversion

The Saracens believe that Our Lord Jesus Christ is the Son of God, but they do not believe that He is God Himself. They believe that He was a superior form of human being, the like of which never was seen before Him, nor is at the present time, nor shall ever be again. Similarly, they accept that He was conceived by the Holy Spirit and born of the Virgin Mary. They hold her

---

39 Luke 22:38.

40 Matt. 12:30.

41 Mark 12:30.

to be holy and worthy of veneration, and the apostles as well. Thus, it is clear that they hold many important things in agreement with us.

We also are able to agree with them, in accordance with reason, upon a great many other points about God—only adding that we believe in the incarnation of Our Lord Jesus Christ. For, this they do *not* believe in. Yet, they do not understand our belief properly, and [they] believe that we believe something that we do *not* believe. For they are under the impression that we believe that God divided Himself into three parts. And one of these parts (so they imagine we believe) descended into the womb of the Blessed Virgin Mary, while another part remained in Heaven, and the third part became the Holy Spirit. And they think that we believe that the part which was incarnate and became man also suffered and died, even in His divinity. These and many other similar errors they attribute to us through their misunderstanding of our doctrine of the incarnation of Jesus Christ.

Therefore, if there were capable men who were able to express clearly to the Saracens what it is that we Christians actually believe and manifest to them the true doctrines which you yourself know well and which

I have endeavored to clarify and demonstrate in my many writings, then through such a means, the Saracens could be readily shown that our doctrine of the Incarnation is not absurd but truly worthy of belief.

The Saracens believe that there is one God only, just as we do. But they imagine (as has been noted) that we Christians believe this one God to have divided Himself into three parts. Nevertheless, they recognize that we, like them, hold to the belief in one God. But they erroneously think that we believe this one God to be formed from, or to be the union of, three distinct Gods, or divine beings. These and many other similar fallacies they attribute to us!

Therefore, if they came to learn what we *truly* believe, particularly in regard to the highest mystery of the Most Blessed Trinity, and if we were able to manifest this to them by means of cogent reasons which no human intellect would be able to contradict, which I have endeavored to present in my various writings in both the Arabic and Latin languages, and which very few of those who follow the creed of Mahomed currently understand—if we could do this, then they would very readily accept our Faith. And once the learned and influential men among the Saracens were convinced of it, then the common people would follow promptly and without hesitation.

The Saracens often assert that we Christians declare our own Faith to be unprovable by means of the intellect or reason. For this reason, they are quick to reject the doctrines we have described above [of the Incarnation and Holy Trinity]. For they do not wish to change their current creed for another which they feel they are being asked to accept on trust alone. Hence it is that our own creed is not held in high esteem among them. In response to this situation, it is necessary that missionaries sent to them should be fully capable of demonstrating that our Faith can, in fact, be demonstrated by reason and supported by sound rational arguments.

Of course, such missionaries need to retain their own personal faith firmly and unwaveringly in their hearts at all times. Nevertheless, for the sake of demonstrating the reasonableness and Truth of our Faith to others, it is necessary that, in discussion and disputation, they be prepared to listen to and engage with other positions with openness and equanimity. Thus, the ideal missionary to the Muslims would be capable of adopting different positions in their own personal prayer and worship of God, in their preaching to the common people, and in rational and philosophical discussion of theological Truths and possibilities. Thus, the intellect of the missionary must be capable of both *ascent* [to the pure contemplation of the mysteries of faith] and of *descent* [toward rational and objective disputation of its Truths on the basis of reason]. Only in this way, and with the help of divine grace, will they be able to prove the Truth of the Trinity.

The Saracens contend that there is only one miracle which is necessary and true, and this is the basis of their belief in the truth of their own law. And the miracle is this: they believe that the Koran was dictated from the heights of Heaven, for they assert that it contains such things that no human being could have possibly written himself. They say that the archangel Gabriel dictated it through the mouth of the prophet Mahomed, and the words dictated in this manner were the will of God Himself. Thus, they declare the Koran to be the very word of God.

The diction and expression of the Koran is indeed eloquent and often beautiful, as I myself can testify. Nevertheless, its content, or material, is false or truistic, and it is adorned with many fables and falsehoods. The so-called miracle of its dictation can easily be refuted, therefore, by the careful refutation or demonstration of errors in its contents.

At present, it does not behoove us to comment on the question of which lord cardinal in particular should be appointed to send forth suitable and properly qualified missionaries for this purpose; for, Your Holiness, this matter is to be commended to your own wisdom and sanctity.

A Description of the Mongols and Plans for Their Conversion

The Mongols,[42] as with many pagan nations, have no real science, nor do they have any fixed or clear creed. They have no definite creed because there is no class of preachers in their society. They have no science because their minds are fully occupied with the daily practical affairs of the world and the things of the senses.

---

[42] Ramon uses the term *Tartar* here but is clearly referring to the ethnic group known as the Mongols. In the thirteenth and fourteenth centuries, after Genghis Khan united several tribal groups into a single strong force, they had established a wide empire covering most of China, Russia, Central Asia, and parts of the Middle East and Europe. The Mongols were heterogenous in religious belief, and Buddhism, Islam, Nestorian Christianity, and animism all co-existed among them.

Therefore, the Church ought to send missionary preachers to them who will instruct them in the holy Catholic law, presenting convincing reasons and sound explanations of our Faith. And not only this but these missionaries should be capable of imparting to them beneficial knowledge of law, medicine, philosophy, and morals.

In achieving the conversion of the Mongols, our own books are very suitable. This is especially so of the one entitled *The Book of the Gentile.* In this book, a Christian, a Muslim, and a Jew all dispute with each other concerning the truth of their respective creeds, while a certain gentile listens to their discussion as a neutral judge. By means of this work of mine, the Mongols will be able to see (if they so wish) that it is the Catholic Faith which possesses the Truth and that both the Jews and Muslims are in error.

When I was in the lands located across the oceans, I once heard that Ghazan Khan, the emperor of the Mongols, was eager to learn more about the beliefs of Christians. And he said that if he could be convinced of its truth, he would become a Christian himself and have his entire army baptized as well.[43] But, alas,

43 As noted earlier, there is evidence that Ghazan Khan had been

there was no one prepared or capable of offering him the clear explanations and convincing arguments he sought! Instead, he, together with all his troops, all became Muslims. This should be a great source of regret and concern to the Church of God and should trouble the heart of every Christian.

Furthermore, once the king of Tunisia, who was a Muslim called Murmiamoli, encountered a certain Christian religious missionary who had mastered Arabic. This religious succeeded in demonstrating to the king that the creed of Islam was false, for this is quite an easy thing to do. The king then said to the same religious: "Now that you have made clear to me the errors and fallacies of our own creed of Islam, if you can convincingly demonstrate to me the truth of the creed of you Christians, then I shall become a Christian myself, and have my whole nation also baptized!"

Now this religious missionary, though well-intentioned, was not particularly expert in philosophy or theology. He told the king that the Truths of Christianity could not be demonstrated by rational argument

---

already baptized as a Nestorian Christian in his infancy. In his youth, he was educated by Buddhist instructors, and later in life, was converted to Islam.

but had to be accepted on trust alone. Upon hearing this, the king was disappointed and said: "I would be very willing to believe your creed if I was given convincing rational arguments of the truth of it. But I am not ready to believe something which you tell me I must accept on blind trust alone!"

Now, if that Christian missionary *had* been able to supply the requested rational and cogent arguments to this king (and such argument can indeed be deduced from the pages of Sacred Scripture and are articulated clearly in my own writings), then that king would have undoubtedly become a Christian, and not he alone, but his entire nation. And if this had happened, St. Louis [IX],[44] the holy king of France, who had then traveled to Tunisia, could have formed an alliance with the king of that land. Together, they could easily have reclaimed the Holy Land. This missionary had a unique opportunity of bringing about the conversion of an entire nation and restoring the Holy Land to freedom, but he had not been given the proper training and resources to bring his work to its fruitful completion and so wasted

---

[44] St. Louis IX, king of France (1214–1270), was a devout monarch who launched the seventh and eighth Crusades. He spent several years in Jerusalem and died in Tunisia.

this chance. The fact that this occurred should weigh heavily on the conscience of all those responsible for this state of affairs.

The Mongols, together with all the other gentile nations, believe that the universe has existed more-or-less eternally. They are also inclined to believe in predestination and place great credence in astrological signs. But the fact that the world has been created, and only relatively recently in absolute terms, is not only clearly established by Sacred Scripture but can also be readily demonstrated through rational arguments. Such arguments are presented in many of my books and, if understood, can scarcely be refuted by any intelligent human being. There is one particular work I have written on the topic of predestination in which it is shown that human beings possess free will and, according to this free will, are capable of choosing to do either good or evil. I have also written a volume on the subject of astrology in which it is demonstrated that the signs observed in the stars are by no means certain indicators of future events.

All of these works would be of great use in converting the Mongols and other pagan people throughout the world. And if they are converted to Christianity, no Muslim will be bold enough to approach them. On the other hand, if the Saracens succeed in converting them to Islam (which, as we have mentioned above, has already occurred in some instances), no Christian will be able to form an alliance with them.

O holy Catholic Church! Do you not see how many enemies you have? Do you not see how many more you *will* have if you do nothing now? For, seventy years have elapsed since the Mongols first left their native land, and already their dominion is greater than that of all the Saracens and all the Christians combined!

Why, therefore, do you sleep, O Church? Why do you not labor to attain this treasure [the conversion of the Mongols] through both the sword of the spirit and the physical sword?

Plans for a New Military Order and New Crusade to Reclaim the Holy Land

Through the angels who dwell in paradise, and through the saints, and through the Holy Roman Church, it is to be earnestly desired that the Holy Land is reclaimed, along with all the other territories which infidels have seized from Christian hands. And therefore, the lord pope and the lord cardinals (since they are leaders appointed for the purpose of honoring Our Lord Jesus Christ and advancing human salvation) should choose one most holy and devout cardinal from among themselves and commit the entire matter of recovering the Holy Land into his hands. This corresponds to our proposal advanced earlier in this tract—that a cardinal should be appointed to establish and govern a new order of missionaries and colleges for their training.

The pope and cardinal should also establish one single military order of knights and appoint their chosen cardinal as head of this order, with the title "Lord, General and Grand-Master of the Holy War."[45] Furthermore, the pope and the cardinals should command and mandate that the Order of the Knights Templar, the Order of the Knights Hospitallers, the Order of the Teutonic Knights, and the Order of the Knights of Calatrava (and indeed all Catholic military orders) should be united into this single new order. For, they are all fighting for one and the same purpose—namely, the honor of Our Lord Jesus Christ and the salvation of the gentiles. If anyone resists such a call to unifica-

---

45 Ramon uses the term *Bellator Rex* ("Warrior King"), but the sense of it corresponds to that of Grand-Master.

tion, then they are neither faithful nor devout! If they fight against this call to unity, they must expect to hear that dreaded pronouncement on the Day of Judgment, "Depart from me, ye accursed, into the eternal fire."[46]

O faithful and devout kings and noblemen (whoever you might be), how much honor you shall receive in Heaven and on earth if you offer your own sons to fight for this great and noble cause! How much will you rejoice and be proud if your son rises through the ranks to an exalted grade in this holy army of Catholic knights! O you who will serve as advisors to the grand-master of this new order, how many laudable aspirations and thoughts shall you nourish toward this noble goal!

O Jesus Christ, come down to us and complete this campaign and bring this matter to its proper conclusion. Lead it to a holy victory! For this is indeed something which only You can do. O Lord our God, may this cause be pleasing to You, which we ask through the intercession of Our Lady, Blessed Mary Ever-Virgin, whose true Son You are. We ask this also through all the angels and saints in paradise, to which innumerable holy souls will come through this Holy War, and

---

46 Matt. 25:41.

through which many souls of sinners shall be able to escape the torments of hell.

The Rule of This New Military Order

The grand-master of the crusade will need to have a rule for his new military order, which we shall now speak about. Firstly, I advise that whatever has been found to be effective in the rules of the existing military orders should be retained and incorporated. Secondly, the new rule should contain whatever is judged by the pope and the cardinals to be expedient and proper.

I will speak now about the cross of this new Catholic order of knights. It is good that the cross should be red in color, signifying that the very first cross was colored red with the blood of Christ. And, indeed, the color red moves the heart and the blood to courage and valor. This was figured in the cross on which Christ died, which was the first cross of the Christian Church and the exemplar and cause of all other crosses.

And because Christ bore His cross upon His shoulders, it is fitting that the cross of this order of crusaders should be figured on the back of the shoulders of their tunics, and similarly on that of the grand-master of the order. It should be positioned in such a way that the transverse arm should be perpendicular to the neck of the soldier.

And because Christ suffered on the cross in His two natures (that is, in His human nature and in His divine nature), it is fitting that the cross should be of two palm spans in length and two palm spans in breadth. And because in the cross, in another way, the three modes of the suffering of Christ (that is, divine, spiritual, and physical) are symbolized for us, it is fitting that the arms of the cross of the order should be of three fingerbreadths in width.

The arms of the cross should be at right angles, just as they were in the first cross. In this way, the cross will be straight and direct. The cross of the grand-master of the order should be the same as that of the soldiers, both in design and size.

The cross of the order should be displayed not only on the tunic of the soldiers but also on their shields and within their lodgings so that the brethren of the order may immediately recognize each other when they see it. It should likewise be visible upon helmets and be displayed on flags. Its size should be adjusted according to the flag on which it is depicted, while its proportions should remain unchanged.

Such is the cross, and such is its placement, figure, and color under which victory in battle shall be attained! For, it is like the first cross through which Our Lord conquered death and the devil.

It is read in the blessed Gospel that when Our Lord Jesus Christ died upon the cross, "darkness came over the earth."[47] The expression *darkness* here signifies shadow or blackness. Thus it was that the first cross, which was colored red with the blood of Christ, was visible against a black background, as it stood erect in the darkened sky. And so, the red cross of this new military order should be depicted upon a black background.

Indeed, the wearing of a black garment signifies those who are in mourning for a beloved kinsman. And those who are in mourning often permit their beard to grow to great length. For, this reason, the brethren of this order of the Holy War should wear a black tunic (bearing a red cross, as described above) and should also wear long beards. In this way, they will signify their sadness and sorrow (and that of the grand-master) concerning

---

47 Matt. 27:45.

the loss of the Holy Land. For, this Holy Land was formerly under the dominion of Christians and has now tragically been seized by unbelievers, and it is to repair this mournful loss that these knights shall fight.

Moreover, the color black is able to sustain stains and dirt better than any other.

And the colors of red and black contrast strongly and strikingly with each other and, when placed together, have an effect of remarkable beauty. Let the habits be properly sized and well proportioned and display the design and colors we have outlined above.

The first cross—that on which Our Lord Jesus Christ suffered and died—represents for us both humility and glorious victory. This humility is expressed by the soldiers of Christ in obedient accordance in intention and thought. And the victory will be grasped only through the same unity of heart and soul in their noble purpose.

And because Christ Himself did not disdain to seat Himself in the midst of His apostles at the table of His last supper, so ought the table of the grand-master be the common table of all the brethren of the order. And this table should be properly ordered so that the grand-master occupies the central place.

The grand-master will need to have counsellors and advisors, for it is good that any questions and motions be addressed with the best possible advice available and only after due and careful consultation with expert, experienced, and devout men.

The Twelve Advantages of the Christians in Fighting the Holy War

There are twelve ways in which we Western Christians[48] excel the Saracens and the other unbelieving nations in conducting warfare. These offer twelve powerful advantages, which should be utilized wisely to ensure our victory.

The first of these advantages[49] springs from the hope that the pope and the cardinals will select a devout and strong cardinal to serve as grand-master of the great new order of Christian knighthood (just as we have proposed earlier) and to act as supreme commander in

---

48 Llull uses the term *Latini* here to refer to Western Christians.

49 The term *modus* ("mode" or "way") is used in the original throughout, but since Ramon is referring specifically to "ways in which Christians have an advantage," it has been translated as "advantage."

the crusade to reclaim the Holy Land; this should be done for the ultimate purpose of honoring and glorifying Our Lord Jesus Christ. For, if the Church, and all Christians, apply their very best efforts to honoring and glorifying Our Lord and God in this campaign, it is only right and just that Christ Himself will be our helper in this war. And if He is, we may be absolutely confident that it will come to a swift and successful conclusion. The powerful and invincible help of Christ, which is just and proper for the Christian side of this war, is something which the Saracens do *not* have. For they are fighting against the supporters of Christ, just as long as they remain in their error.

The second advantage is this: if the grand-master of this order should be Christian to his very heart and has an ardent desire to achieve victory for Christ, then many other noblemen who are like-minded will join his army. They will willingly support themselves with their own funds and resources. This is something which is not possible for the Saracens. For, among the Saracens, their fighting men are typically not wealthy. Compared to the Christians, they are mainly poor in material resources and therefore unable to fund themselves to form and sustain their army in a way that the Christian nobility can easily do.

The third advantage will come from the willingness and capacity of the grand-master of this Holy War to apply himself continually to the campaign of battle, waging the crusade without cessation or intermission. If this is done, the Saracens will very soon fall into despair, for they will begin to believe that the war will last forever and their resolve will weaken and fail. And if the grand-master of the order should die, another should be selected immediately to take his place. And if any of the soldiers of the crusade should die, another member of this Catholic military order should be ready to fill his shoes. When the Saracens witness this happening, they will conclude that this great holy army will never be able to be overcome and is inexhaustible in its resources and unstopping in its persistence. It will then not be long before they give up their efforts of resistance and take to flight. In this way, the Christian forces will soon succeed in driving them from the Holy Land and reclaiming it for the dominion of Christendom.

The fourth advantage which the Christians will have in waging this war is that our forces will consist of well-trained and well-equipped men. In this respect, they will be much superior to our adversaries. For our own soldiers will be governed by the rule of their order of knighthood and constantly practicing the arts of combat and living in a disciplined manner. Moreover, they will possess the courage which springs from faith. The Saracens, on the other hand, have neither the organization and structures in place nor the funds available to form an army of comparable skill, discipline, or resources, as our own certainly will be.

The fifth advantage which the Christians will have in any war against the Saracen hordes is this: our horses and skilled horsemen, who are able to wield weapons with skill while mounted upon their beasts, and who will be fully equipped with helmets, spears, and shields. The Christian cavalry will also be a refuge and protection for the grand-master of the army, which the Saracens will not be able to overcome or infiltrate. For the Saracens are not skilled in mounted warfare or horsemanship in general, nor do they use protective armor on their bodies. And they are neither expert in the use of shields nor in fighting with spears.

The sixth advantage which we Christians possess is the science of firearms,[50] and we have mastered especially the use of these weapons by mounted soldiers. The Saracens lack the science and art of firearms entirely and use only bows with which to launch projectiles of any kind. And in battle, firearms always excel bows, and therefore Christians may count this as a very powerful advantage.

The seventh advantage for we Christians is not only the fact that we have firearms but that we should become capable of using them to the maximal extent and in the optimal way. The wood which is used in their construction grows in the lands of Christendom, but not in the territories of the Saracens. The grand-master of this Holy War should undertake to have many armed soldiers. Those who are foot soldiers should make use of larger firearms of two feet in length. For the Saracen soldiers will not be able to remain standing when confronted with such weapons. Furthermore, I propose that our armed infantrymen should be equipped with strong shields, and thus protected. [As has been

[50] When Blessed Ramon was writing this (1311), firearm technology would have been extremely new in Europe. His knowledge of this reflects his keen interest in the natural sciences.

noted,] the Saracens do not have the practice of protecting themselves with shields but go forth into battle as if they were uncovered.

The eighth advantage we have is the fighting abilities of the Almogavars.[51] These are foot soldiers who are very skilled with the spear and shield, who can attack from near or far at either day or night. Great numbers of these Almogavars are available from Catalonia, Aragon, and Castile. Such a multitude of swift, skilled men is necessary if we are to acquire the Holy Lands, and therefore the grand-master of the crusade would do well to recruit a great many for his army.

The ninth advantage which the Christian forces hold is our deployment of siege engines and other machines of war. For the Saracens have neither the type of timber available which is necessary for the construction of such devices nor do they know the method of using them, as we do.

The tenth advantage which we can bring into play is the maintenance of long sieges against the cities and

---

[51] The Almogavars were light infantry soldiers originating from Aragon. The name is derived from the Arabic word *al-mughāwir,* meaning "the raider." They participated in the ongoing Reconquista in Spain against the Muslim Moors.

military encampments of the Saracens. The better resourced our army is and the greater the abundance of provisions available to our troops, the greater will be our ability to besiege the foe for extended periods of time. And this is something which the Saracens will not be able to withstand or to match.

The eleventh advantage of the Christian forces is our superior command of the seas. For we far surpass the Saracens in our ships and navies, as is obvious.

Finally, the twelfth advantage we Christians will enjoy is that our access to provisions and supplies is far more abundant. As well as our naval forces (which the Saracens lack), we have access to iron. Now, the Saracens have the ability to travel and convey goods only by land, and they have no reliable access to iron, as they depend upon that which they happen to acquire by chance.

Because of the twelve advantages which are described above, I contend that if a suitable grand-master of a military order dedicated to the waging of this Holy War were appointed, we Christians would be able to attain dominion over all the lands and territories of the Saracens and other unbelievers. And, therefore, whoever is appointed to such a role, or whoever will be appointed to such a role, should have confidence in his ability to succeed under any circumstances. We conclude here with what seems to be an apt expression: "Let him who has ears for hearing, hear!"[52]

The Saracens, however, have three particular advantages over the Christians: One of these is in discipline and order-of-command, which their soldiers observe, and the good regimen of their armies. Another is the use of the Turkish bow.[53] The third is the great skill they have in archery and their mastery of this art in war. But the grand-master of our forces will be able to provide a remedy for each of these.

Regarding the first (the good ordering of the Saracen armies), we could achieve a similar thing by appointing one commander over every ten men, then another commander over each hundred, and another over each thousand, and then another over each ten thousand. This structure of command could continue even until a million soldiers were covered! And whoever disturbed or defied this structure of command should be punished most severely.

---

52 Matt. 11:5.

53 The Turkish bow was able to launch arrows over a very great distance.

Regarding the second and third advantages possessed by the Saracens (the use of the Turkish bow and skills in archery), our own soldiers could be specially trained in this art and also learn the use of the Turkish bow. This would be a wise thing to do. For in this way, the skills of the Saracen fighters as archers would be met with matching skills from our own forces, and thus cease to be an advantage for them.

Through the cultivation of all the advantages that the Christian forces enjoy over our Saracen adversaries and that we have outlined above, the grand-master of the crusade would, with the help of God, certainly attain ultimate victory for Christendom!